samsoon adventures ❀

samsoon adventures ✿

samsoon adventures ✿

samsoon adventures 🌸

Fall, Winter with Samsoon

samsoon adventures 🐾

samsoon adventures 🍀

samsoon adventures

Author's Note

Hello!

I am grateful to share Samsoon along
with your Korean learning adventure.

The workbook involves practicing Korean words (Hangul)
and coloring Samsoon Adventures illustrations.

I hope the coloring adds a place of solitude to take breaks
between your Korean learning exercises.

I want to thank and acknowledge my mother,
who encouraged me ever since I could grab a pencil
and have dreams of my own.

I hope the Samsoon Adventures workbook motivates your learning process, like
how my mother encouraged me at every step
of my creative flow.

Dream on!
With love & light,
Soon Ju & mother

samsoon adventures ✿

samsoon adventures 🌸

samsoon adventures 🐾

samsoon adventures ✿

samsoon adventures 🐾

Dedicated to

samsoon adventures 🌸

samsoon adventures ✿

samsoon adventures❀

가을

1 - 3

samsoon adventures❀

가을

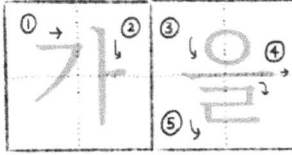

(gaah-eul)

autumn

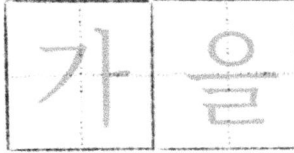

가 을

축제

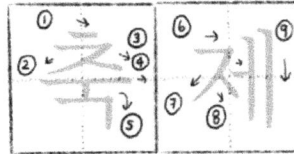

(chook-jae)

festival

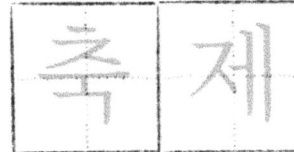

축 제

춤

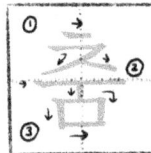

(choom)

dance

춤

samsoon adventures 🦋

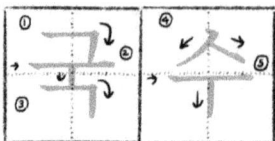

(geuk-soo)

noodle

(gaam)

persimmon

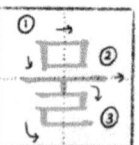

(mool)

water

받는것

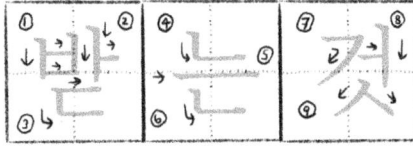

받는것 (baat-neun-gut) receiving

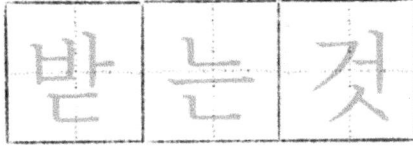

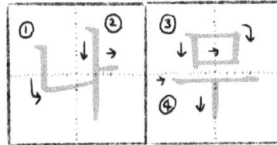

나무

나무 (naah-moo) tree

은하수

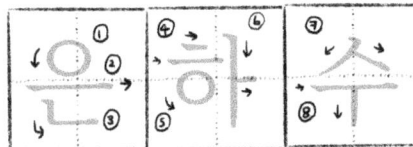

은하수 (eun-ha-soo) galaxy

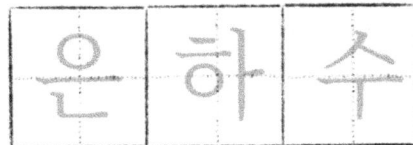

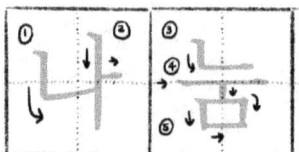

나눔 (nah-noom)
sharing

나 눔

사랑 (sah-rang)
love

사 랑

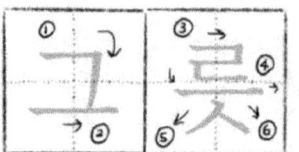

그릇 (geuh-reut)
bowl

그 릇

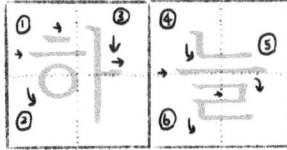

(ha-neul)

sky

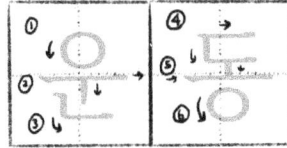

(oon-dong)

exercise

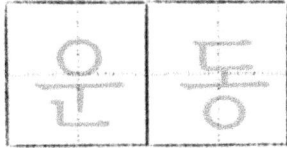

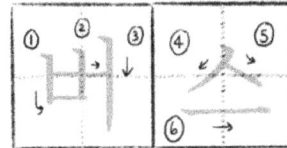

(buh-seu)

bus

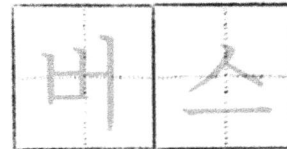

베개

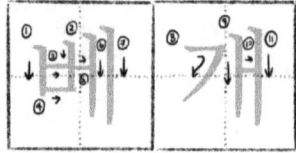

(bae-gae)

pillow

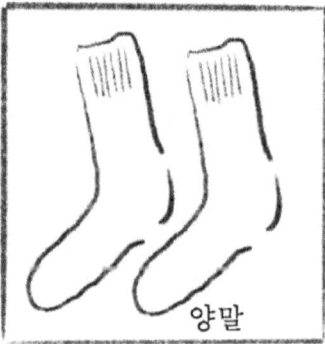

양말

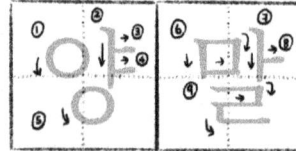

(yang-maal)

socks

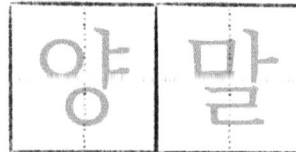

가방

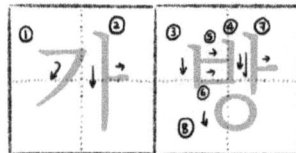

(gah-baang)

bag

기차

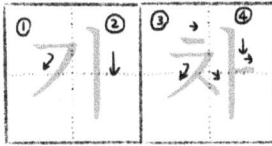

(gee-cha)

train

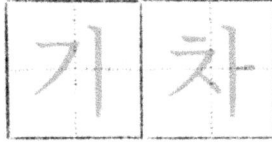

기 차

저녁

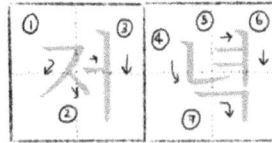

(juh-nyeuk)

night

저 녁

달

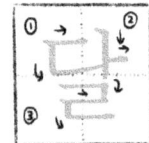

(daal)

moon

달

조상

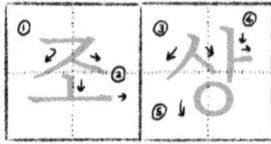

조 상 (joh-saang)
ancestor

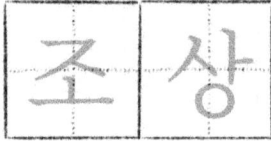

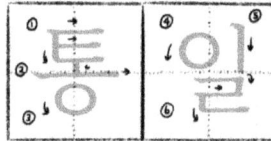

조 상

통일

통 일 (tong-eel)
unity

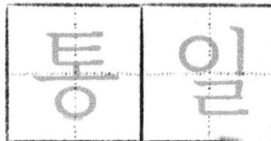

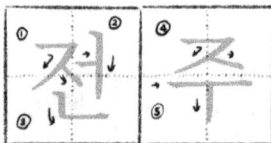

통 일

전주

전 주 (jun-joo)
Jeonju

전 주

떡볶이

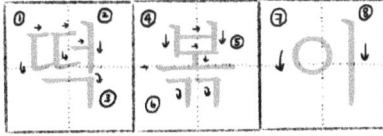

떡 볶 이 (tteok-bok-ki)
Tteokbokki

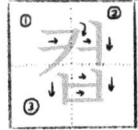

떡 볶 이

컵

컵 (cup)
cup

컵

김밥

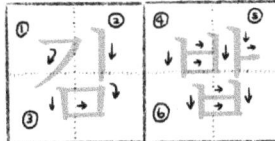

김 밥 (kim-bap)
kimbap

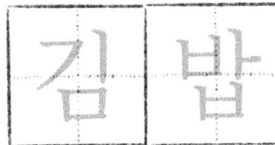

김 밥

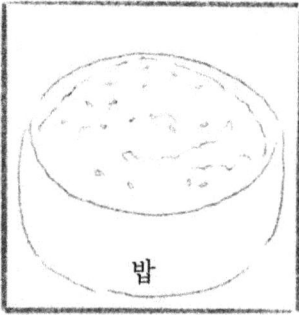

밥

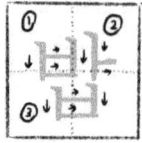 (bap)

rice

김치

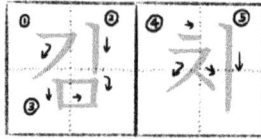 (kim-chi)

kimchi

냄비

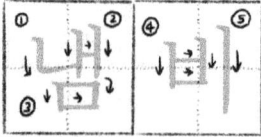 (naem-bi)

pot

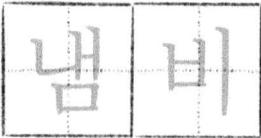

보름달

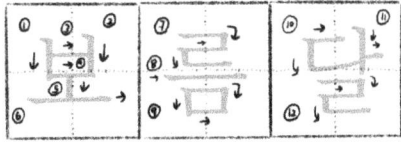

(boh-reum-daal)

full moon

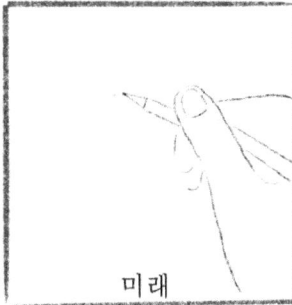

미래

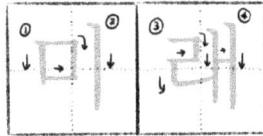

(mi-rae)

future

심장

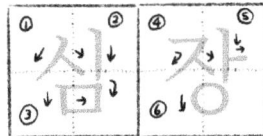

(sim-jang)

heart

산

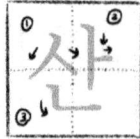 (saan)

mountain

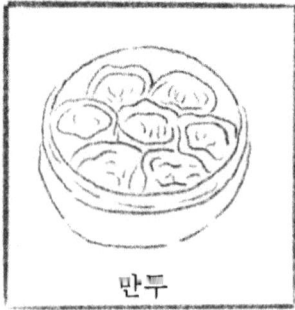

만두

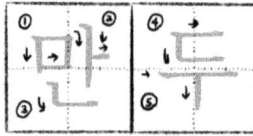 (man-doo)

dumpling

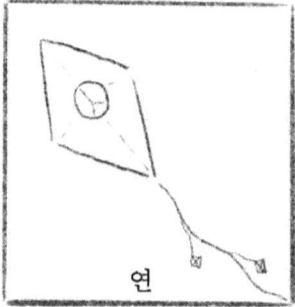

연

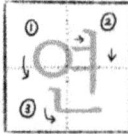 (yun)

kite

껴안다

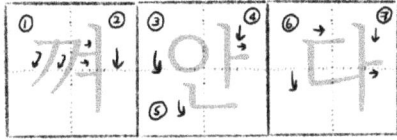

(kkyuh-ahn-dah)

hug

공동체

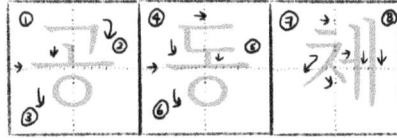

(kong-dong-chae)

community

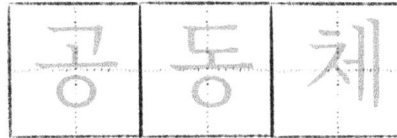

함께

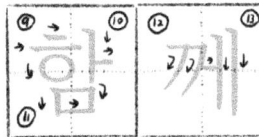

(haam-kkae)

together

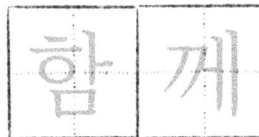

우물

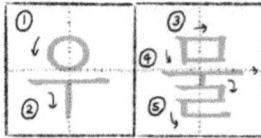

(ooh-mool)

well

우 물

나뭇잎

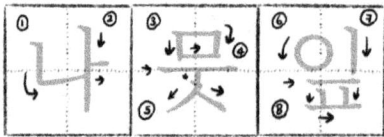

(nah-moo-ip)

leaf

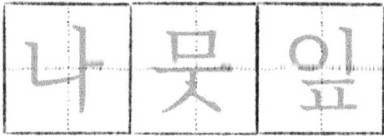

나 뭇 잎

별

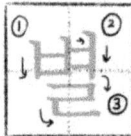

(byul)

star

별

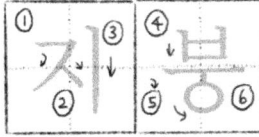

지붕

지 봉

① 지 ③ 봉 ④ ⑤ ⑥ (ji-boong)
roof

지 봉

사다리

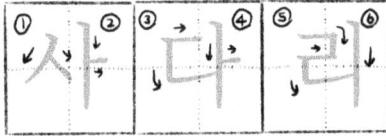

사 다 리 (sah-dah-ree)
ladder

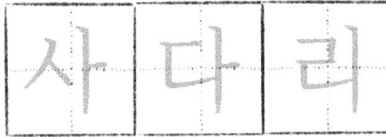

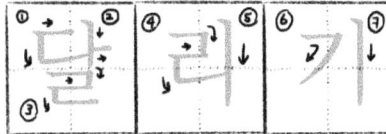

사 다 리

달리기

달 리 기 (daal-li-gi)
running

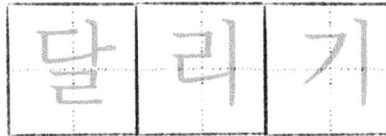

달 리 기

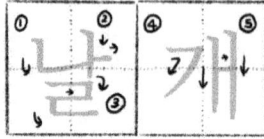

날개 (naal-gae)
wings

날 개

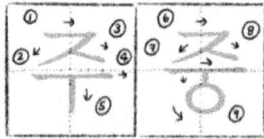

주중 (joo-joong)
weekday

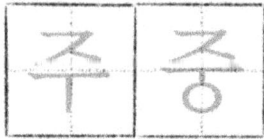

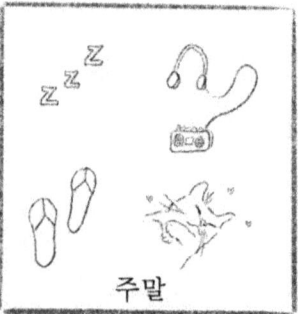

주 중

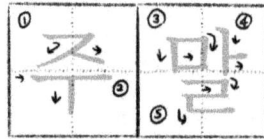

주말 (joo-maal)
weekend

주 말

팀 워 크

팀 워 크

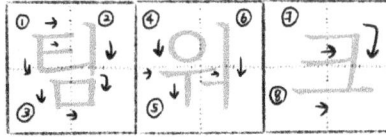

(team-wah-kuh)
teamwork

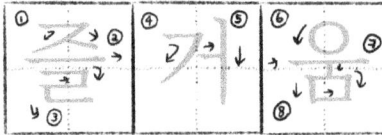

즐 거 움

즐 거 움

(jeul-guh-oom)
joy

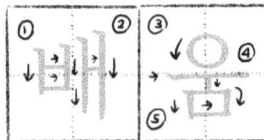

배 움

배 움

(bae-oom)
learning

samsoon adventures 🍀

samsoon adventures ✿

samsoon adventures 🍀

samsoon adventures

samsoon adventures 🌸

samsoon adventures

samsoon adventures ✿

samsoon adventures ✿

samsoon adventures 🍀

samsoon adventures

Samsoon adventures ❀

겨울

 1 - 4

samsoon adventures ❀

겨울

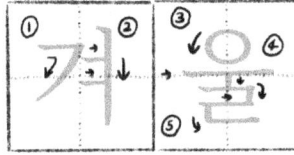

겨울 (gyu-ool)
winter

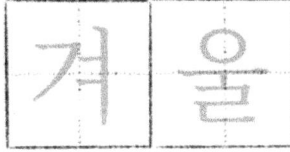

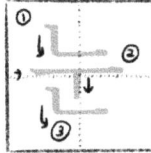

눈

눈 (noon)
snow

파랑

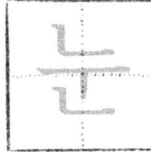

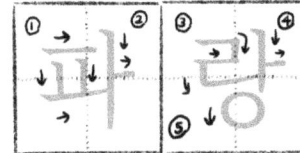

파랑 (pah-raang)
blue

고구마

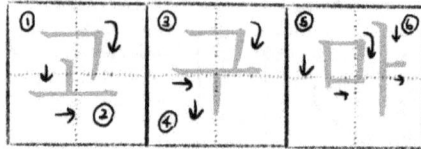

고구마 (go-goo-mah)
sweet potato

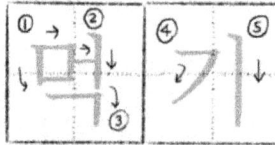

고 구 마

먹기

먹기 (muk-gee)
eating

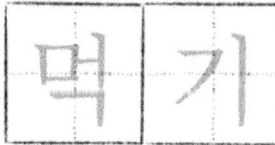

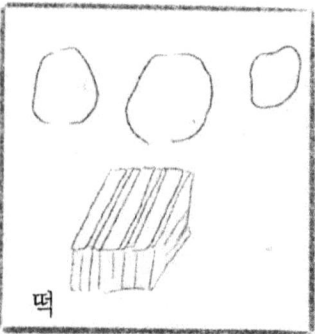

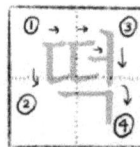

먹 기

떡

떡 (tteuk)
rice cake

떡

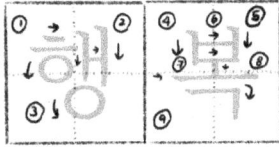

(haeng-bok)

happiness

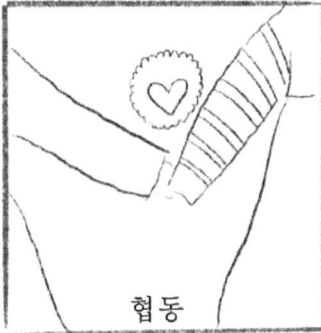

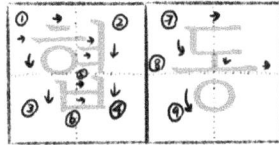

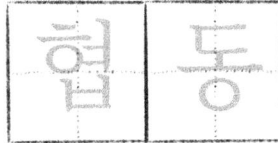

(hyup-dong)

collaboration

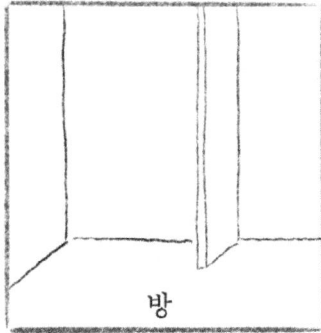

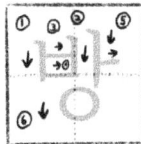

(baang)

room

samsoon adventures

추억들

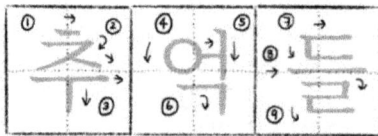

(choo-uk-deul)

memories

추 억 들

바라보기

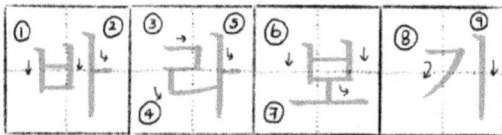

(bah-rah-bo-gi)

to look

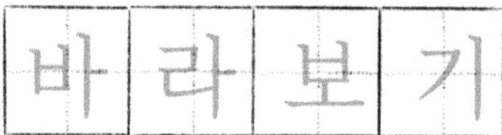

바 라 보 기

친구들

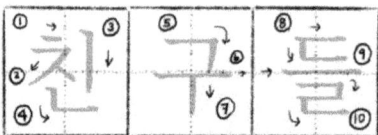

(chin-goo-deul)

friends

친 구 들

계절

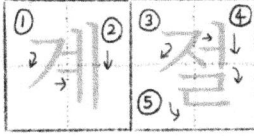

계절 (gae-jeul)
season

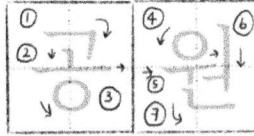

계 절

공원 (gong-won)
park

공 원

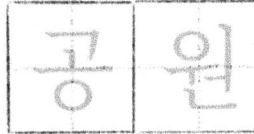

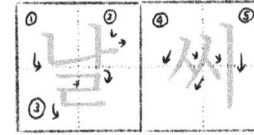

날씨 (nal-ssi)
weather

날 씨

할머니

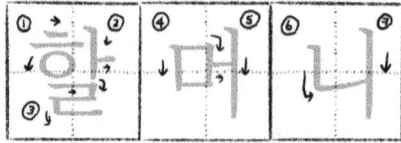

(hal-muh-nee)

grandmother

친구

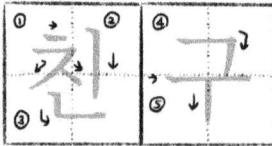

(chin-goo)

friend

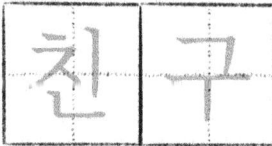

요리

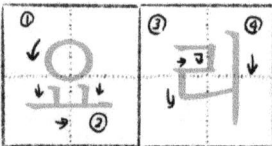

(yo-ree)

cooking

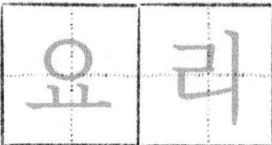

5

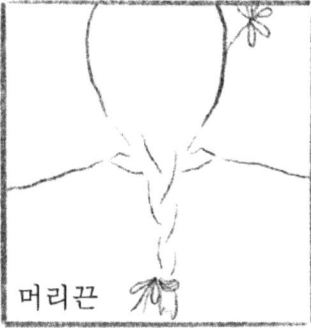

머리끈

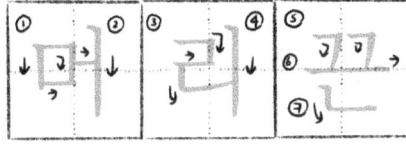

(muh-ri-geun)
hair tie

목도리

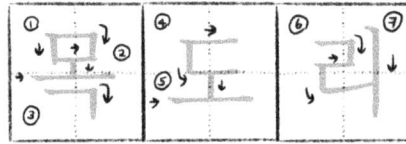

(mok-do-ree)
scarf

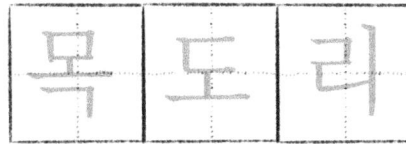

한복

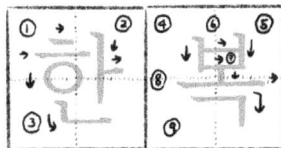

(han-bok)
hanbok

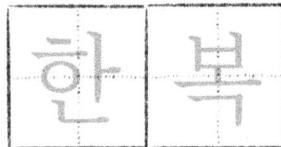

samsoon adventures

조끼

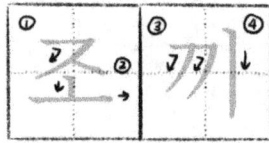

(jo-kkee)

vest

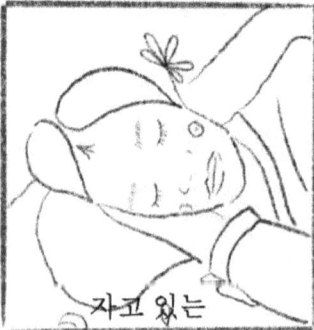

자고 있는

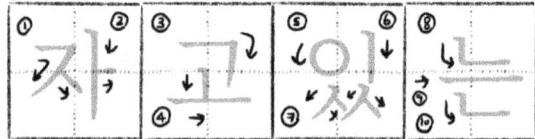

(ja-go-eet-neun)
sleeping

불

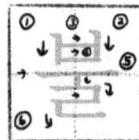

(bool)

fire

불

3

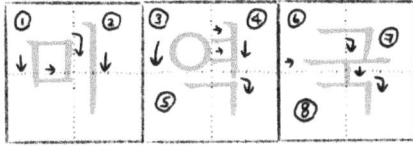

미역국   (mi-yeuk-kook)
seaweed soup

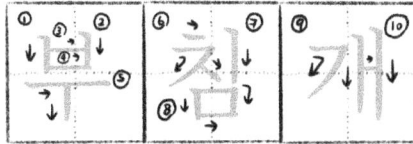

미 역 국

부침개   (boo-chim-gae)
korean pancake

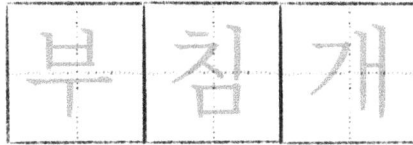

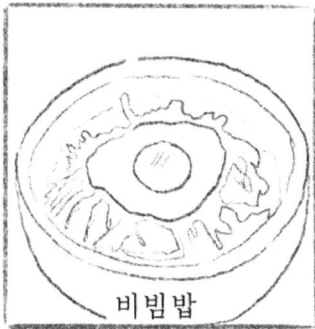

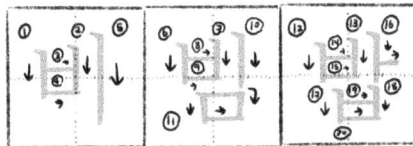

부 침 개

비빔밥   (bi-bim-bap)
bibimbap

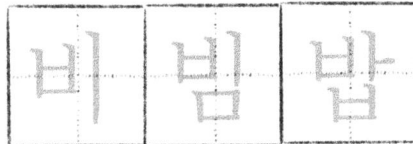

비 빔 밥

솔방울

(sol-baang-ool)
pinecone

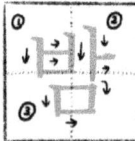

솔 방 울

밤

(baam)
chestnut

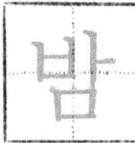

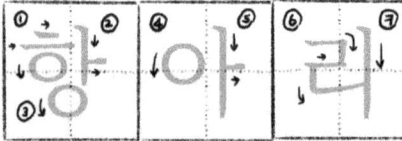

밤

항아리

(hang-ah-ree)
jar

항 아 리

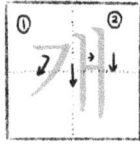

(gae)

dog

개

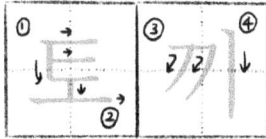

(to-khee)

rabbit

토끼

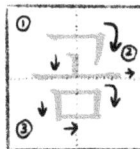

(gom)

bear

곰

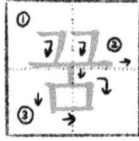 (kkeum)

dream

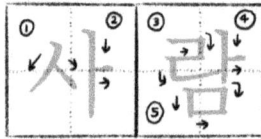 (sah-raam)

person

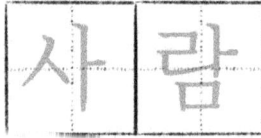

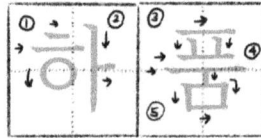 (ha-ppeum)

yawn

말하는

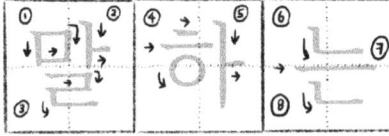

(mal-hah-neun)

talking

볼연지

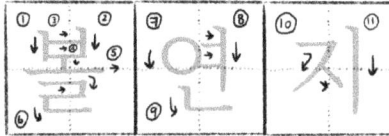

(bol-yeun-jee)

blushed cheeks

나이

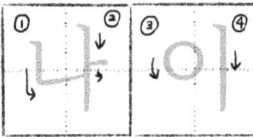

(nah-ee)

age

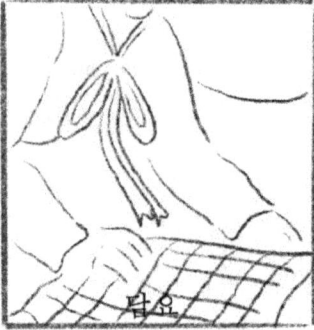

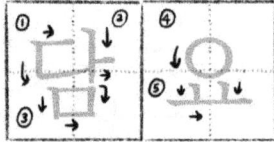 (ddam-yo)

blanket

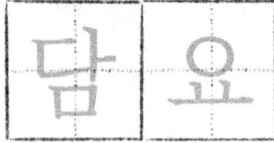

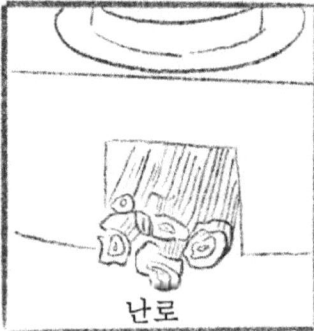

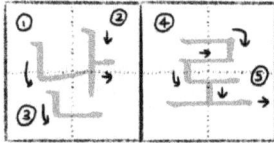 (naan-roh)

fireplace

4

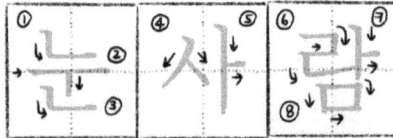 (noon-sah-raam)

snowman

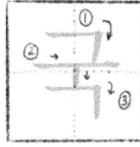 (kook)

soup

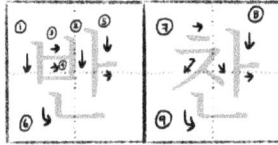 (baan-chan)

side dishes

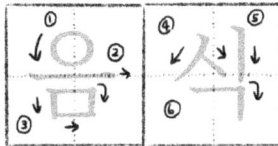 (eum-sik)

food

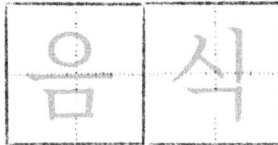

작별인사

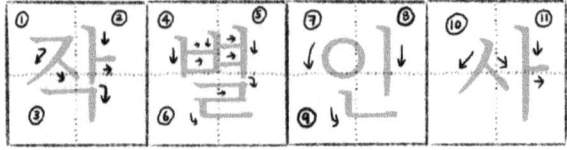

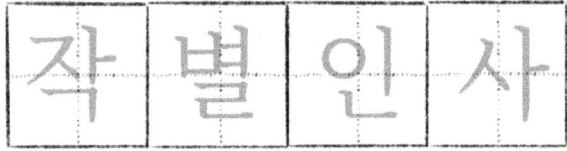

(jak-byul-een-sah)
farewell

도움

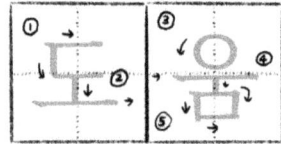

(doh-eum)

helping

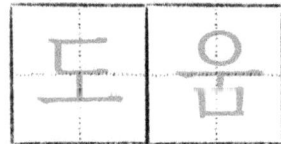

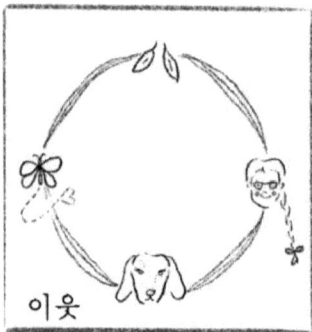

이웃

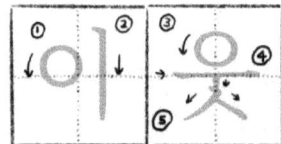

(ee-eut)

neighbor

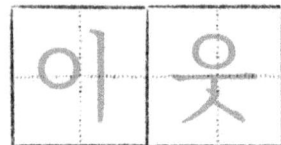

감 사 해

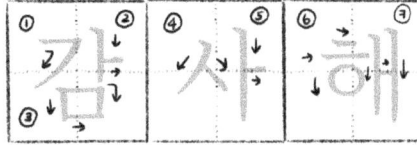

감 사 해 (gaam-sah-hae)
thank you

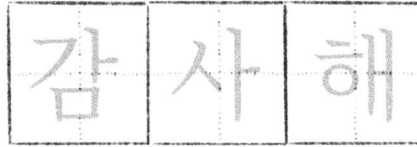

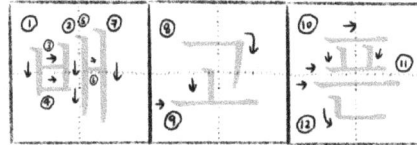

배 고 픈

배 고 픈 (bae-go-peun)
hungry

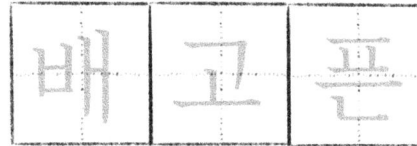

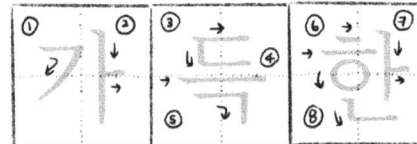

가 득 한

가 득 한 (gaah-deuk-han)
full

samsoon adventures 🐾

samsoon adventures ❀

samsoon adventures ❀

samsoon adventures ❀

samsoon adventures

samsoon adventures

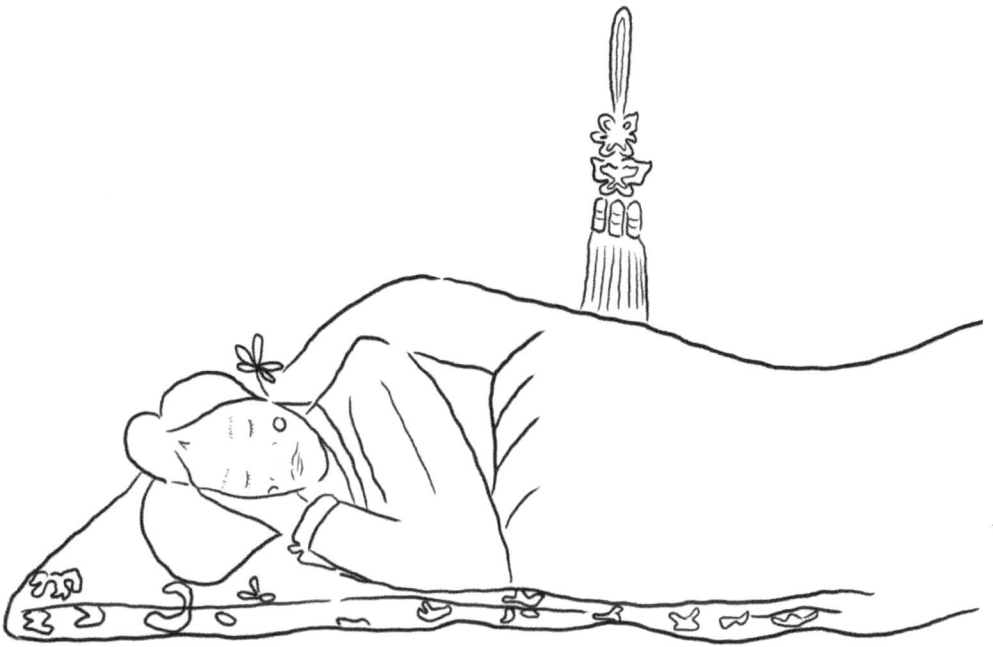

samsoon adventures ✿

samsoon adventures

samsoon adventures 🍀

samsoon adventures 🐾

samsoon adventures

samsoon adventures 🍀

samsoon adventures ❀

samsoon adventures🐾

Samsoon Adventures

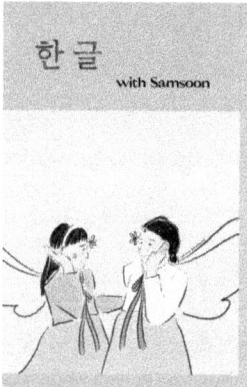

Hangul with Samsoon

 Write your daily Korean sentences with a square-style notebook, suitable for all ages!

Recommended for beginners, with dotted squares inside.

Flowers with Samsoon

Immersive Korean self-learning flower exercises for all ages, with easy how-to-pronounce, how-to-write steps provided.

Samsoon Adventures

Another Day, Another Blessing

Write down your self-guided, self-oriented daily to-dos, gratitude, and reflections.

Mindfulness productivity design inspired by Korean time wheel.

Cultivate an ever-blossoming self-purposeful garden! How-to use provided.

Samsoon and Farewells

Written and Illustrated by
Soon Ju Kim

Samsoon and Farewells

Samsoon and Mimi were best friends, finding joy in everyday experiences with their Grandma.

One day, Samsoon faces the reality of departing from her best friend.

We learn with Samsoon the beauty of departures and how to overcome them gracefully.

samsoon adventures ✿

samsoon adventures ♧

Samsoon Adventures

www.ingramcontent.com/pod-product-compliance
Lightning Source LLC
Chambersburg PA
CBHW020908100426
42737CB00045B/1214